Kaiso 4 Kids

Alex Bruno

A book by ALEX BRUNO
Edited by Anaya Bruno
With Preface by Anaya Bruno and Illustration by Errol Evelyn

First Edition

ISBN: 978-0-99157283-0

Typesetting G & D Enterprises Inc

The Lost-generation Heritage Series (L-GHS)
Book 1
About the Lost Generation

The lost generation represents a predominant Caribbean mindset which is mainly demonstrated by individuals who had not made the shift to the cultural trends of the times, instead they hold on to traditions with the misguided notion that by so doing, they are indeed embracing and celebrating their culture. The issue is, however, that tradition is not culture and vice versa, so that prevailing attitude keeps those who subscribe to it caught-up in a sort of false Caribbean limbo.

This Caribbean limbo is found in the lost generation's attitude towards politics, spirituality and religion, culture and traditions, other traditions and global issues, development, customs, interpretations, conceptions of leadership, responses to leadership, the attitude towards past and emerging generations, and most importantly, creating a stalemate in the link of progress from one era of Caribbean reality to another.

Examples of people who inhibit the traits of the lost generation would be the appreciation of one type of music Cadence, in the Dominican context. This view expresses a standard benchmark for that music as being a particular rhythmic pattern which does not, or should not evolve. Those from the lost generation are slow in adapting to new and creative ways of cultural evolutions, they harbor a quasi-colonial mindset when it comes to practices and traditions, they maintain a sort of a mental block towards differing attitudes and ideas of Caribbeaness and progress, and they display disdain for challenges to their Caribbean disposition.

In my view, the lost generation is a Caribbean phenomenon. This is the case because the lack of indigenous construction, or founding, of the region. The lost generation generally encapsulates people between the age group of 36 - 56. People in that age bracket were born into a region, in the late 60s to mid-late 80s which was characterized by an attitude of reform and resistance. Those who reformed did a bit better than those who resisted.

Resistance here means an anti-reformist attitude, and not resistance in the sense of pushing back against artificial notions of who we are as Caribbean people. In other words, the term 'lost generation' describe those who have/did not truly appreciate what the Caribbean is or was, or what it can become.

This L-GHS, which comprises of 4 separate books (Kaiso 4 Kids, Kadanse 4 Kids, Kwéyòl 4 Kids, Kulture 4 Kids) serves as a necessary spark of awareness. I believe it will assist in provoking the children to think beyond that lost generation gap in our Caribbean consciousness. These books are not just for Caribbean audiences; they are meant to embrace global attitudes of Caribbean traditions and culture, and to connect Caribbean children with others of different regions.

Alex Bruno

Preface

Reading through this book, I found it very entertaining and relatable for young, curious minds – such as my own – and very eye-opening to the importance of culture, and keeping it live through continually passing down and practicing tradition. The dialogue between the two characters of the story (Benoit and Gil) bring the story to life. The writing cleverly engages readers to think deeply and critically about calypso and Carribean culture.

I'm sure that this book will teach many children – both Carribean and non-Carribean – to embrace and appreciate their culture through their roots. I really enjoyed the story, I found it highly entertaining and funny, and Benoit asks so many questions until he finally understands, just as I do.

Anaya Bruno

Introduction

The word 'kaiso' is an acclamation, like Bravo! Rooted in African customs, the word was used to express satisfaction about powerful expression of literary and performing art. The Caribbean is the birthplace of Calypso. In fact, since Calypso landed on the West, following the atrocious journey of enslaved Africans across the Atlantic, it has been one of the most potent forms of expressions.

Calypso, therefore dates back to the mid-15th century, and during the early days , the chant of 'Kaiso' would be shouted out whenever Calypso fans felt like the Calypso punchline. Kaiso is an acclamation of the part of the Calypso message, or hook, which resonated with the people. In fact, Kaiso became synonymous with Calypso to the point where both words were used interchangeably to describe the same performing art in song.

What is Calypso, anyway? Well, that is what this first book in The Lost-generation Heritage Series (L-GHS) is about. Without delving too deep into the waters, this book introduces readers to one of the world's musical genres which probably evokes the most passion from the people who perform it and/or are affected by it. Calypso was never meant to be entertaining, but it quickly became an entertainment art so that it would be received by the society of people who needed to hear it.

While we remain on the shallow side of the water in this book and series, readers are encouraged to read 'HISTORICAL PERSPECTIVES OF CALYPSO AND SOCA MUSIC IN DOMINICAN CULTURE – Dominica Music, A revolutionary Trend' for deeper insights into the making of Calypso. The objective is to present a launching pad for deeper inquiries. I am of the firm view that much more focus should be placed on children if a more progressive world is going to be realized.

This series targets children between 8 – 12, or children of any age; even younger and adult children. There is something for every one in the L-GHS.

This first book is dedicated to the memory of Slinger Francesco aka The Mighty Sparrow.

Alex Bruno

Calypso is Art

Calypso is Culture

Calypso is Intellect

Calypso is **Storytelling**

Calypso is more than Music

Calypso is a way of life of a **People**

Calypso is the voice of the Voiceless

Gil & **Benoit** discuss all of the above and

more...

Read the book ☞

Look out for Book II — *Kulture 4 Kids*

Gil is chilling on the big stone. He just had his usual recreational substance, and he started blenching out some classic calypsos...(Singing)

"...Dan is de man, in de van. Can a pig dance a jig for a fig? Twirly and Twisty were two screws. Mister Mike goes to school, on a bike. Dan is de man, in de van. Dan is de man, in de van Yeah! Dan is de man, in de van!"

Benoit, who was wondering by, heard Gil singing. He walked right up to Gil and said: "But Gil, the thing gone-up in your head man? Can a pig dance a jig for a gig? What are you really saying...what is that?"

Gil exhaled and said: "I am singing a calypso song that your grandfather used to sing before your mother was born."

Then he proceeded to sing; "Can a pig dance a jig for a fig." Benoit was not amused; "this is simply ridiculous, as my teacher would say," he replied and asked Gil to pause his singing for a bit.

After taking his seat next to Gil on the big stone, Benoit said, "I wish I knew papa. As you keep saying, he was a wise man who made a lot of sense, but that song you were singing there...

it does not make much sense. Can a pig – Gil cut him off sharply and exclaimed: "Everything that Sparrow, the undisputed Calypso King of the world, has ever sang makes sense; you just have to make sense of it, Benoit."

The MIGHTY SPARROW

The Calypso King of the world!

Benoit, still a bit bewildered, looked at Gil and asked him: "Please help me make sense of the pig dance a jig for a wig thing." Gil replied; "I sure can," but Benoit still insisted...thinking to himself...

"...but how can he make sense of something like that thing which is not even in style again?" And Benoit said, "As you said, Mr. Gil, Calypso is my grandfather music."

Gil responded by saying, "and that is where you are wrong; Calypso is not just your grandfather music, it is our great, great, great grand fathers' music."

"Wow!", Benoit exclaimed, "You are making things worse.
"How so?" Gil asked.

"Well, you said that Calypso is 4 times not in style; it is our great, great, great grand fathers' music", Benoit insisted and advised that new music forms evolve with every generation.

At this point, Benoit is pacing frantically and his gesticulations are have become more pronounced.

"How can the old be new, and how could something evolve and still remain the same, Gil?

"Have a seat, Benoit," Gil replied, "and listen well". Gil picked up his box guitar which was leaning against the big stone and started strumming away at the strings: "Calypso or Kaiso is an unchanging traditional art," he says. "What makes Calypso, Kaiso is the element of resistance and fight which is trapped in the very creation of the music."

"Please break it down; keep it simple" Benoit yelped in frustration, as he paced again and prepared to leave.

"Calypso, by its very nature, is an evolutionary art, Benoit." Gil places the guitar in his right hand and taps on Benoit's shoulder. "Calypso evolved from the people pain."

Before Benoit could get out the question 'which people?' Gil stated that "Calypso came from the Africans' struggle; the Africans who were captured from the continent, transported to the West, and enslaved."

Benoit whispered an inaudible quote which served as affirmation for Gil to carry on. "It is the enslavement of the people and their new reality of struggle, anguish and oppression which caused the birth of Calypso," Gil explained.

"It is the feeling of despair which fuels the Calypso rhythm, and as long as that feeling persists, Calypso will continue to evolve as an extension of the people's heritage."

"Oh, I see," Benoit muttered, "so the sense of evolution is the spirit of Calypso?"

Yes! Yes, you got it right, Benoit...that's it - exactly; the sense of evolution is the spirit of Calypso, you could not have stated it better."

Benoit who got a burst of empowerment by Gil's statement, leaped onto the stone and began sharing views while asking additional questions about Calypso. So, is Calypso and Kaiso the same? When was Calypso first created and where? Why is Sparrow the Calypso King of the world? Is Calypso a Black music?

Is Calypso African or Caribbean? Why is Calypso part of the people's heritage or tradition, and what does heritage, or tradition mean anyway? With a green, Gil responded as follows: Calypso and Kaiso mean the same; Calypso actually means to conceal, and Kaiso is an affirmation - like bravo! Calypso was created when the peoples' despair began - right on the Atlantic crossing.

Slinger Francesco aka 'The Might Sparrow' is undisputed king because there is simply no one, alive or dead, who have represented and presented the artform quite like him."

Gil further explained that Kaiso is neither Black nor White; "it is liberation music – the voice of the downtrodden," he explained. "Calypso is like a tree which grew from African roots and bears Caribbean fruits," said Gil. With a gentle pause and brisk nod, Gil concluded that "Calypso is traditional because it is part of the people's way of life – it evolved from their struggle, and if you want to know about traditions and tradition, I suggest that you read this book", and with that, he handed Benoit a book titled: Kulture for Kids.

There was sort of an awkward silence before Benoit could take the book from Gil. It was as if Benoit had other questions.... many more, and this allowed Gil to get one more point in.

He said, "Benoit, probably the most important thing you should know is that all the countries of the Caribbean adopted and practiced Calypso, which though might be peculiar to the particular country, was not owned or discovered by the country; so, it simply is not true that Calypso was born in Trinidad & Tobago."

Benoit said, "Oh ho," and he calmly walked away.

THE END

Kaiso: A Definition

The art of rendering Calypso belongs to no one, and no institution or country can claim to have designed or even developed its blueprint. Calypso is instead the freedom to practice a creative form without borders. Thus, Calypso can be defined as a form of musical expression unleashed on the world by Africa, through the struggles of its Caribbean descendants.

Calypso is unconquerable and eternal. It cannot be suppressed, lost or stolen. It cannot be reconditioned or reformed because it is a natural and perfect aspect of a people's 'Africaness'. It is a highly sophisticated form of intellectual expression in song, which was developed by Africans to communicate the ills of the capture and the system of forced labour or enslavement of Africans.

Intellect, as I understand it, is the faculty of objective reasoning. It is what helps the individual to decipher abstract or other academic matters from others and triggers an understanding or mental analysis of the effective powers of a case, person, and/or group(s) of individuals, or thing. Intellect is beyond education; in fact, it teaches education to understand itself. This is what Calypso is; intellect.

Calypso has its own basis (the people), and point of reference (the peoples struggle); it informs and regulates itself based on the human's desire for justice. Any engagement involving Calypso is, therefore, an intellectual pursuit which is the hallmark of academia. The art form took shape across the Atlantic by the rhythmic chants and call and response, led by Calypso panaceas that induced others into verbalizing their mental anguish.

The mask, a way of saying something to mean something else, was used to ensure the safe delivery of the
message. Upon arrival on the plantations in the West Indies, the "enslaved" Africans seized their freedom by unleashing their rebellious expressions that had already been highly developed across the Atlantic.

But the realities of the new endeavour gave definition to the form; Calypso gained added punctuation and punch, and such punches are laced with pun and satire, as earlier discussed.
Calypso comes from the nucleus of a people's identity, and it took slavery to bring it to life in the way that it has evolved.

Calypso was strengthened by the hundreds of years since that era, and it will continue to strengthen every time there is injustice or oppression. Calypso was not conditioned by the societal order; it made a shortcut through the onward leg of the Triangular Passage and landed in the Caribbean as its own unique entity.

Calypso has remained intact, strong and undefiled and it now serves as a 'socially acceptable' dagger in the side of the oppressor or evil doer. No one is immune to Calypso, not even the calypsonian.

www.ingramcontent.com/pod-product-compliance
Lightning Source LLC
Chambersburg PA
CBHW042107040426
42448CB00002B/178